Learn how to invest .. in stocks

Tables of content

Chapter 1.

Introduction

In this book you will learn how to invest in stocks for short term and long term as well and make money in the process.

Do it yourself ...yes don't trust your money with some mutual fund guy and why not if you can do it yourself with less than 20 mins in a week all you need is a good strategy which we will learn here and sound discipline should make you successful.

Believe me you can do better than most professional investors with right risk management and properly following the plan.

Now if you are tensed oh now he is talking all Greek words , so don't worry just stick with this book till the end and you will have your diploma in investing in stocks.

Hi I am parag chude and I am full time trader and investor I also invest other people's money I am research analyst.

I am in stock markets from last 13 years and I also had same problems what you as a beginner must be going through so I thought of writing a book for those who don't want to leave their full time job but still want to participate in stock markets.

So in this book you will learn one simple investment strategy. Which will make you profitable and will help you achieve better performance than your current mutual fund scheme .

So without wasting further time lets move ahead ....

Are you excited and willing to learn????

CHAPTER 2.

The tools you need

So I will try to make it very simple all you need to have is a D-mat account with any good service broker I will recommend you open your account with service broker and not a discount broker.

Most retail investors like you and me have inclination to save the brokerage and we tend to lose sight on the bigger picture of better service and long term survival.

So don't be penny wise and pound foolish.

But if you wanted to save that brokerage part you can open your account with reputed discount broker also I don't have any issues.

A good broker and charting software with end of day data is sufficient, don't worry if you don't know how to read a chart like a pro.

I will teach you to find very simple methods and very clean

charts . also ill tell you where to look for free charting data

Some of the websites mentioned below gives data free try them

Investing.com, tradingview.com or chartink.com

You can use any one of them but try to stick to only one so you are comfortable with it for understanding and clarity I will use investing.com charts in this book .

So after opening your d-mat account you need funds to put in the account if you are beginner I suggest you start with very little funds at the start as this is your learning period and you may do some mistakes which will cost you money .

So start small , if you are already in markets and know the know how's you can start with whatever amount you are comfortable to put aside at least for one year period as in this book you will learn strategy which will take in consideration one year period .

So you need charts like shown below

This is daily candlestick chart of Tata Steel

Note how it shows price history in candlestick chart pattern

How the price is all over the place in selected periods .

But as a investor you need not be concerned about this volatility as you will learn the technique to avoid any price falls and on those times of crashes you will be out of the market with your money and of course your profits smiling and waiting for your next opportunity.

Second thing you need to understand is

Moving average indicators –

A moving average is nothing but a line drawn on charts which is made of closing price data of last selected no of candles

For example

A 200 period simple moving average is nothing but a line drawn on chart which is nothing but closing price of last 200 days

Like here shown in chart.

200 dma shown in this same chart which is blue line drawn on

chart .

We will need other moving averages as well ,there are many types of moving averages we will be using simple moving average and nothing else as I believe in keeping things simple .

Some other moving averages are

20 dma (Dma is day moving average)

50 dma

100 dma

200 dma

Different traders use different moving averages its like which size of shirt suits you and fits you that matters

We will use

10 DMA

50 DMA

200DMA

And from now onwards we will use only these moving averages for our further studies and investment purpose .

And with my 13 years of experience I am telling you , you need simple strategies to win with stocks .

So after placing all moving average your chart will look like this

As shown below

10 DMA is green in color

50 DMA is red in color

200 DMA is blue in color.

So now your chart will look like this

This is your master chart and you need to follow only this charts for your investment purpose.

Isn't it very simple ??

All you need to do is check in your favorite list of stocks or your invested stock list daily for 10-15 mins and check if any new action needs to be taken or not and you have to relax and count your money in bank

See all endeavor is to make you confident so you can win in this game of investing..

You can make returns like 24%, 45% 78% 12%, 102% and like wise and your losses will be very small like below 10 % and that's my friends is the secret to stay in this business forever.

What most retail traders do is hang on with their losing positions and cut their winning positions too soon thus missing the whole picture .

You need to do different to win this game and its very long term game so once you start making money like this you will also use compound interest in your favor. And you can make huge wealth for yourself and your loving family .

Another requirement is capital (seed Money) you need starting capital in this game of investing I will equip you with the necessary knowledge but you have to come up with capital .

So that's it you need charts money and moving averages to make you rich

If this is so simple then why everybody is not doing this ???

In this game of investing you are your biggest enemy. Its you who will not allow you to prosper .

If you are new I request you to only follow this method and keep learning but follow only profitable methods in stock markets.

Its not important to be right always in markets but very important to be wrong small.

So whenever you are winning win big and whenever you are losing lose small it's the Holy Grail friends.

You follow any strategy but keep this in mind always ..

So ill show you what I mean

Trader A

Stock 1	+ 8%
Stock 2	+7%
Stock 3	+ 9%
Stock 4	+11%
Stock 5	-79%
Stock 6	-89%
Stock 7	+3%
Stock 8	+7%

He is winning in 6 out of 8 trades but winning small and losing in only 2 trades but losing big

So what you thing is his total performance ? if he has invested in equal amounts in all the stocks 10000/- each his total returns are -12 % on overall capital with 80% success rate he is losing money yes you heard it right .

Now lets look at trader B

Stock 1	-5%
Stock 2	-8%
Stock 3	-9%
Stock 4	-2%
Stock 5	+72%
Stock 6	+52%
Stock 7	+36%
Stock 8	-7%

So what you think with only 3 winning stocks out of 8 that is 40 % winning ratio how he is doing ???do the math's ......

He is actually up in his account 13 % . so that's the trick win big when you win and lose small when you lose .

If you promise me that you will do only this in investing my purpose of writing this book is achieved .

Don't waste time learn this once and for all and you will be winning trader and investor in your community .

But people hate to lose all you need is psychology to celebrate your small losses that's why 90% of people in stock market lose money friends

So now do you want to be in 90% club or in 10% winning club choice is yours ...

CHAPTER 3
The strategy

So now the main part the strategy which will make you rich

In any strategy you need three things

The entry

The exit

Stop loss

So we will look each one by one

The entry rules ---

Whenever 10 DMA crosses 50 DMA from below we will buy stock .

Like shown in this chart 10 DMA which is green line crossing 50 DMA which is red line from below we will buy this stock next morning at market open.

The exit rules

Whenever 10 DMA crosses 50 DMA from above we will sell out stock

As 10 dma which is green in color crosses 50 dma which is red in color from above we will sell our stock the next morning at opening of market.

Its this simple friends but very difficult to follow as our own greed and fear will come into picture

So now what is our stop loss

Whenever our averages tells us to exit the stock we will sell it ,simple .

So if we buy today at 100 rs because 10dma crossed 50 dma from below and in 2 days 10 dma crosses 50 dma from above we will sell our stock incurring small loss .

And if the trend goes higher we will have tons of money its that simple ....

But now is the time to add another rule

As this is buy only strategy we will come to hunting markets only specific times ..

Yes guys only that special time of the markets what people call Bull markets or buying markets

We will not do any activity in Bear markets or falling markets

Isn't it cool to just be safe with your money outside markets waiting for our right opportunity to strike .

Believe me worlds all professional investor does this though they might be suggesting you to buy and hold stocks or your favorite mutual funds .

Don't fall for that trap

Okey now the rule

We will only trade our strategy in bull markets i.e. your general market index like Dow in US in India we have nifty is above its 200 DMA .

Yes simple addition

See below nifty chart with 200 DMA added to it in blue color you would have so well by staying out of markets and in cash whenever the markets break 200 DMA.

That's the key your general markets should be in uptrend for you to do well with this strategy that's actually the 1 st rule

Note in chart above green arrows shows the times you should follow this strategy with your stocks and blue arrows shows break of 200 DMA and you should be out from markets with your money safe in banks.

And the stock which you are selecting for trading investing should also be above 200 DMA line

So now the market is bullish the stock you are trading is also bullish

And you will buy on 10/50 crossover so timing is correct so there are no chances left for any errors.

This is our strategy which we follow with our own money and with our clients money serving us well over a long periods of time .

And if you also do it you will be in 10% group of people earning money.

CHAPTER 4

The psychology needed for winning investor

So now you know what needs to be done

1. You need bull market (index above 200DMA)
2. You need stock in Bull markets(stock trading above 200DMA)
3. You will buy if 10 DMA crosses 50 DMA from below (10/50 Crossover)
4. You will sell if 10 DMA crosess 50 DMA from above (Reverse 10/50 crossover)

Example

Note in above chart

Stock above 200DMA (BULLISH)

Buy cross came at 2410 (Green Arrow) NOV 2018

Sell Cross came at 3452(Down arrow) July 2019.

Posting gain of 43.24% absolute gains in period of Nov 2018 to july 2019 only in 8 months less than a years time .

Is it not cool gains ???

You can do this

Yes believe me you can do this ...

Lets look at some other example s

Now look at reliance which is frontline stock buy cross (green arrow) came at 910 on 08-06-2018 and sell cross (red arrow) came at 1210 on 03-10-2018 so again in less than year only in 4 months you could have earn 32% that too in frontline stock .

Now I know you must be getting greedy and thanking me for sharing this magical strategy with you .

But there wont always be winning stocks you will have fair share of losers but all small

Remember I told you to keep losses small and wins Big

So if you can do this consistently
You will make big in stock markets
That's my promise to you but you need to be disciplined to follow this religiously then only you will taste success.

Now let's see how you may lose also

So above chart
Buy @ 1140 on 29-11-2018
Sell @ 1106 on 07-01-2019
Loss of -2.98 % in 2 months period

Now do you get what I am talking

Keep losses in check and you will fine in stock markets .

Nobody tells you this how to do it part

But I am helping you so you don't lose your hard earned capital and earn money for your family .

I know its just one simple strategy but this can change your financial life forever.

Trust me you will beat all mutual fund managers and all hedge funds doing this .

CHAPTER 5
Risk Management

This is Holy Grail of investing

Risk management is science of staying in the game many novices will not follow risk management and will lose all their precious capital believe me I lost all my initial capital because there was no one to tell me this.

Now ill tell you what exactly needs to be done

Suppose you have 10 lakh starting capital

Divide it in 10 parts or 20 parts so make 10/20 different blocks of money and buy 10 different stocks following our strategy.

This way you are not risking too much on one single stock or one single market operation.

This is fairly simple risk management to follow.

Now you can take on the next Bull market head on and start making money .

Don't forget me send me your blessings and ill be happy for you .

Don't overtrade
Don't try to take opportunity every other trade

Keep learning other methods try my other books on daytrading
But follow only this method for investing..

CHAPTER 6
The plan

Have a plan to compound money.

If you can compound your money 20 % annually you will beat Warren Buffett in longer run

That's magic of compound interest.

Follow my other Books where I have discussed this concept in detail but for now keep in mind to double you invest ment every 3 years and in 10 years make 10 time your original amount .

So in next 10 years 10 times will take you to 100 times of your original investment so have 20 year plan.

Don't think short term follow long term plans

That's the plan you need to follow you can do this its very simple but difficult to follow .

If you have that spirit to do the needed may god bless showers of wealth upon you .

CHAPTER 7
Do it yourself......

NOW A FINAL NOTE

You can do this the confidence much required I have given you think for your own future and future of your family .

Don't trust your money with any body .
Its your hard earned money invest wisely

With strategy discussed in this book you should do fine over longer term and with no stress whatsoever

That's a big plus over others .

If you have any feedback difficulties reach me at paragchude@gmail.com and I will be happy to help you if you are interested to learn with me send me mail and I will share with you various programs that will make your trading and investing to newer heights .

As I always say this is just beginning

All the best to you !!!!

Thank you for reading this Book....

www.ingramcontent.com/pod-product-compliance
Lightning Source LLC
Chambersburg PA
CBHW030603220526
45463CB00007B/3163